MANAGING OUR SELVES:

God In Our Midst

ELIZABETH POWER

E POWER & ASSOCIATES
1992

FOR INFORMATION, CONTACT:

E POWER & ASSOCIATES

P.O. BOX 2346

BRENTWOOD, TN 37024-2346

For those led to believe that their abuse was sanctioned by God;
Their multiplicity purely from the enemy of God;
and whose dignity has been stripped from them by Christ's believers.

For those in the Body of Christ who wound others from fear,
Who do not know or will not know the horrors others have endured.

For those who believe that we who have endured
know no truth and have no light in us,
calling us liars
rather than remembering the practices of Baal and Molech
which surely continue
both inside and out of the Christian Church.

May God restore us all.

ACKNOWLEDGEMENTS

Firstfruits are important: to God be the Glory. I am God's, more and more, all of me.

To those who have read, edited, and wrestled with me on the content, I am grateful. Dogma and doctrine are fatal errors: Scripture should be sufficient, and relying on it as a foundation is the only hope for overcoming denominational "isms."

To those in my childhood who helped nurture spiritual development of all sorts-- for without them all, I would not be where I am now. The influence of the many traditions I have followed and the many paths I have walked have helped forge the beliefs I now hold and they are all part of God's refining.

I thank especially Dr. Jim Friesen, author, clinician, and Fuller Theological Seminary faculty, Rev. Robert Kohler of the United Methodist Church's Board of Higher Education and Ministry; and Dr. Ray Elder, director of Nashville's Life Challenge and a long time proponent of the national Teen Challenge program. These three have read and re-read, edited, suggested change.

My new-found friends counted among women clergy, Rev. Patricia Lewis and Rev. Beth Richardson (both of the United Methodist Church), and Rev. Blair Both and Martha Honaker (from the Episcopal Church), I was helped to wrestle (no angels involved here!) with content and theological issues. Had we all been lucky enough to meet across all the state lines involved, they, too would have read and re-read; as it was, I bent their collective and individual ears a great deal for ideas and perspective.

These readers and supporters represent the breadth of Christian tradition. I learned a lot from all of them. I also thank the many multiples with whom I have spoken who cry in the night for acceptance and forgiveness, who struggle with who they are in the spiritual realm, and who long to feel a sense of belonging in the Church which represents the Body of Christ.

And, to the many whose homilies have touched a chord, my thanks. Especially to Peter Outzs of St. James' Episcopal in Lenoir, NC, for a sermon connecting the concept and ideas of the personal Jerusalem.

Refreshing. Hope-embracing. Challenging. Engaging. Truth-seeking. Affirming. These descriptors fit all of Elizabeth Power's work, especially "God In Our Midst."

People can scrap. Denominations can joust. Selves can quarrel. But that is a lesser way. "Blessed are the peacemakers, for they will be called God's children." That is what this book is about--bringing peace without sweeping honest questions under the rug. Questions like, "Where was God when I was growing up?" and "What is God's position about abuse?" need careful consideration. Thank you, Elizabeth, for you careful examination of some principles that promote peace, inside and out.

Jim Friesen, Ph. D.

CONTENTS

MANAGING OUR SELVES:

God In Our Midst

ELIZABETH POWER

This book comes out of my own personal journey. It is imperfect, as I and my journey have been and are. In many ways it is piles of stones I have set as altars, like the ancient Israelites, along the way in those places where I have had a deeply personal encounter with God.

There is, for us who are multiples, the potential for the greatest hope and the greatest rejection in the community of Christians. We who call ourselves-- the selves we know of in our selves-- Christians face the inevitability that there may be selves in us that are **not** Christians. Those parts of us may have yet to hear or be moved by the message of Our Lord and Savior. Parts of us may feel too much judgement and shaming by the Church to embrace Christ. Other parts may wish nothing to do with the whole matter, finding power in other theologies. Yet others may doubt, disbelieve, or think it foolish.

The Church-- Christ's representative-- beckons, yet rejects. It says "Come unto me, all you who are heavy laden and I will give you rest, as long as.." and the rules begin. We are told we are welcome, conditionally. For what reason? Our need for hope and the horror in our lives far exceeds the limits of "normals." The horrors which we have endured and in which we have participated are unspeakable to the eyes of almost every person: they are what I call "concentration camp experiences," or our own private Vietnams. They are without social validation; and we are, after all, "mentally ill." We are told our lives are stories unable to be heard except by clinicians (who often become hardened or burn out from hearing them) or, perhaps, privately, by Our Lord Himself. We are to pass as "normals" or to pass on to other places.

And thus it is that while it is God who offers us our only lasting hope in healing, it is God whose representatives offer us fear and rejection. My anguish is deep over these matters. I am sure that this is not what the Jesus of the Gospels intended. I am sure that Jesus does intend that neither we nor those around us victimize each other with and by our lives, either through spilling them over and over in their darkness to each other **or** by denying their existence.

This is the second workbook in the "Managing Our Selves" workbook series. Each workbook can be used independently of the other.

Just as with "Building the Community of Caring," you can't get "rid" of any sense of self or anything in your past.

You can, however:

1. **Explore ways of thinking** about Christian spiritual life that are comforting, reconciling, and help you heal.
2. **Add information, attitudes and skills** (helpful only if you practice them) that may make your journey easier and help you have more "up time."
3. **Choose to consider, adopt as your own, or discard the ideas.**
4. **Increase your ability to respond** to other selves and others as Christ would, thus furthering the kingdom.

Some folks without the label MPD find the ideas interesting and even useful as Sunday school materials. They do have broader application if you choose to see them that way.

At the MPD/DD Resource and Education Center, we want to know if and how this workbook helps you. We develop materials for all segments of the community, make presentations and speak to many people about MPD. Your comments and feed back will help us to be of better service. Please write us at P.O. Box 2346 Brentwood, TN, 37024-2346.

Here are some pointers about how to get the most out of this workbook.

Remember that many of you may read it-- and may read it over and over again. Some may like it, some may not. That's ok.

It opens flat, so you can put it in your lap.

There's **lots of room** around the words so everyone can make notes for each other.

The **sections are short**, so it's easier for everyone to read, and so that if you're switching a lot, you have a better chance of getting through a section. It also means you can use short blocks of time to pick up the work book. work with an idea, then think and pray about it for a while-- and respond with how you think and feel about it over time.

There are **questions** for every one along with each section. There's a place where each of you and all of you can make your own response, so that as different selves read the same material, they can respond. It helps every self see every one's point of view-- and while they may be different, they're all important.

You can **open the work book anywhere** and begin. It's ok to skip around.

Feel free to **cross out words that bother you** and **substitute synonyms**. I find that keeping a Thesaurus to look up words that trigger me is helpful: it gives the words less power over my life, and I am actively choosing to take that.

Denominations: organizations representing groups of congregations. How did they start? When early Christians traveled to areas where there were no churches, each church formed was self-administering. As churches began to multiply, one of the ways to preserve what some felt was the "true" church was to form legislative and administrative bodies to which area churches belonged. While the body of Christ is one, the forms which the body takes are many. Each one claims to be a part of Christ's Body and each one claims to know the "truth" of the apostolic faith.

Dogma is the body of doctrines, or beliefs, concerning faith and morals to which a denomination adheres. Individuals adopt these beliefs as their own point of view, often with more than a little variation.

How do denominations and dogma fit in this workbook? There is no way to write to accommodate the varying differences between denominations and the dogma to which each of us adheres. There is a way to look at what we all have in common, and that is what this book focuses on.

For example, while not all Christians believe the same way about holidays, all Christians believe in the same Jesus Christ-- there was, after all, only one Jesus and two thieves at Calvary. There is not a separate Jesus Christ for each denomination.

In general, denominations find that the Bible is the basic source for information regarding spiritual matters, so this workbook uses Scripture as its reference and point of departure.

Please-- read for your selves. Ask God to give you wisdom in knowing what to believe and how to use what you read. Read around the parts that vary from what you believe, and remember that I, too, am still growing.

May God the Father, Son and Holy Spirit--and all the feminine aspects of God as well-- make plain what is yours to understand and protect you from anything not of benefit to you in this workbook.

What do you believe about the role of the Holy Spirit in your spiritual growth?

With which Christian denominations are you familiar, or to which have you belonged?

How might different denominations as parts of the body of Christ be like different selves with our self?

We all long to be saved. To be freed from, rescued, delivered, defended avenged of the wrongs done us is a natural yearning. It is also a yearning rooted in our desire to be safe from the wrongs we have done.

The people of Jesus' time had gotten a little weary of waiting for their deliverer, seeing as how some of the folks they knew who lived in right relationship with God and with their neighbor still suffered-- anxiety, pain, even torture and death. They rather thought of salvation as a matter for the world after life where everyone would get their just desserts-- suffer here and have it good there.

Jesus didn't play into the needs of the people then, or of us now, to have it that way. When he was asked "Will only a few be saved?" he didn't answer as expected. He didn't single out anyone. He talked about how the door was narrow, and how we will be surprised by who is and who is not there (Luke 13:23-25). He was saying, in a way, look for and take hold of every chance you see to strengthen your personal commitment, to seek and obey God's will for you, in spite of how it looks or feels.

His model for us in this is in his sorrow over Jerusalem (Matthew 23:37). The experience in Jerusalem was exactly what God had called Jesus to do. If he was to look for and take hold of every chance to strengthen his personal commitment, to seek and obey the will of God, he had to go on. His salvation as a human was dependent on His embracing what he knew he would do in Jerusalem, no matter the cost. Our salvation was dependent on his!

We each have our own Jerusalem. In many ways, our personal salvation involves embracing, as he did, the pain and suffering of our past-- instead of wallowing, fighting, or complaining; embracing and accepting it. We, like Jesus, can transform the evil conditions of our lives by "turning our faces towards Jerusalem" and going there, admitting our grief about the pain it brings and going deliberately and willingly to the glory it yields through our obedience.

Our darkest moments hold the hope of the greatest glory when we are willing to seize them, whether wrongs done to us or wrongs we have done. So it was for Our Lord, and so it is for us.

How is your past like the Jerusalem to which Jesus went? What did he face there?

What choices were available to Jesus about Jerusalem, or what could he have done to save Himself from the crucifixion?

Read the story of the Garden of Gethesemane (Matt. 26:36-46; Mk. 14:32-42). Describe how you think Jesus must have felt about what he knew lay before Him if he was obedient to God.

How is that like what you feel about obedience to God, especially in facing the Jerusalem of your own healing?

The word "trinity" means threefold. In Christianity, it refers to God the Father, Son and Holy Spirit as three persons in one. God the Father and Spirit are described many times in many ways in the Old Testament, and prophetic writings about God the Son are found there also.

God the Son and Spirit are New Testament themes, with Jesus Christ always deferring to the Father and pointing to the Spirit. The baptism of Jesus in the gospel of Matthew (Matt. 3:13-17) describes Jesus, the Spirit of God, and a voice from heaven proclaiming Jesus as "my son." In the stories of the temptation, Jesus refers to himself as "the Lord your God" (Matt. 4:1-11).

The gospel of John speaks to the Trinity in many places. Read the following references to find out what John says about the multiplistic person of God:
John 1:1, 18
John 3:11, 34-35
John 5:17-22, 26, 30
John 8:19, 58
John 10:30, which lists Deuteronomy 6:4 as its reference
John 13:31-32
John 14:8-11
John 15:26
These verses give a picture of the relationship between the three persons of God. They are all God, yet are all separate: each operate as co-conscious expressions of the Self of God.

Even though our multiplicity is as a result of trauma, it seems to me that if it is a holy expression of the Self of God, to the extent that Jesus even speaks of Himself as "we," that there is inherent value in it-- not in the abuses which cause it, in the ability to have multiple aspects of self with different functioning.

Perhaps once we resolve the trauma that caused our multiplicity, have fluid flow of information instead of amnesia, have agreement instead of conflict, and aspects of self operating more in the harmony modeled by the relationship of the trinity, we will be more conformed to Christ.

What does your denomination believe about the trinity? If it does not believe in the trinity, how might this information still be useful to you?

If we are made in God's image, what is the difference between the multiplicity expressed in scripture and ours?

What is the difference between "integration" and "conformity to Christ" as goals for healing as they relate to the concept of the trinity?

It's easy to read the Bible one way and one way only, whether it's to isolate verses that seem to condemn or approve. Chances are that for every idea from Scripture in this work book, you can find an opposing idea right there, too.

For example, when you read about the concept of the Trinity, you have room to say that the idea of the unity of God is missing. And you're right, there is no section on the unity of God.

Why? Well, I figure most people, and most selves, have heard concepts and ideas that are **not** in this work book, and few have heard of or read the ones that are. Another example is the concept that follows, talking about "One Body, Many Parts." You can read the verses used as references, and then turn around and you can find as many in the opposite direction.

Each of us multiples faces choices about how we believe about ourselves and about God, and about how God might believe about us. I know that I am painfully aware of the condemnation and judgement God might pass on to me, and I am much less aware of the mercy, comfort and love. I see too readily the places where Scripture, doctrine, and dogma separate me from the love of Christ. Much more hidden are the experiences for me, my selves, and I of the similes God has inspired man to record where I, in my selves, may find comfort and hope.

And so I risk "proof-texting," knowing that there are selves that could argue Scripture till the sun breaks again into daylight, telling me that one is incomplete without the other. So it is.

And just as we multiples could not live as a single self without the many selves, neither can either side of a set of verses exist without the other-- otherwise, they both would not be in the Book! Therefore, instead of selves arguing over what to include and exclude, remember to keep it all in balance.

As we live as symbols of Christ's love, remember His life and the process of His healing us is also symbolic.

How do you feel when someone takes one verse from the Bible and tries to make it more important than any other, especially if it condemns you?

What do you think about the importance of reading and believing equally the verses that approve of who you are becoming as a person grounded in Christ?

Since much of life may have asked you to believe lies about yourself, how is it to consider believing God's truth and love for each of you, regardless of what you have done?

What would it take for you-- all of you-- to begin to believe each self and all selves are important to God and cared for by God?

Paul, in his writings to the early Christians, talked about the parts of the body as parts of Christ, just like multiples have part selves that make up the self of the body. Here's what Paul said:

"Just as each of us has one body with many members, and these members do not serve all the same function, so in Christ we who are many form one body and each member belongs to the other" (Romans 12:4,5)

"The body is a unit, though it is made up of many parts; and though its parts are many, they form one body. So it is with Christ. For we were all baptized by one Spirit into one body--whether Jews or Greeks, slave or free--and we were all given the one Spirit to drink.

"Now the body is not made of one part, but of many. If the foot should say, 'Because I am not a hand, I do not belong to the body,' it would not for that reason cease to be part of the body. If the whole body were an eye, where would the sense of hearing be? If the whole body were an ear, where would the sense of smell be? But in fact God has arranged the parts of the body, every one of them, just as God wanted them to be. If they were all one part, where would the body be? As it is, there are many parts, but one body. The eye cannot say to the hand 'I don't need you!' And the head cannot say to the feet, 'I don't need you!'(1 Cor. 12:

We each represent one physical body. Just as we have different parts of the body, we also have different part selves. When Paul writes to the Ephesians, "For he himself is our peace, who has made the two one, and has destroyed the barrier, the dividing wall of hostility.. His purpose was to create in himself one new human being out of the two, thus making peace, and in his body to reconcile both of them to God through the cross, by which he put to death their hostility" (Eph. 2:14,16), I hear his voice speaking to the part selves that would war with one another.

Each part is as valuable as the whole. Each self was created because of pain. The conflict and chaos that some carry are not who they are; those characteristics are representative of the pain from which they were created. Teach all the concept behind selves as part of a body, connected as God would have it connected--warts and all--and whose peace comes through nurtured relationship with God.

How is each part of you, even the selves you don't particularly care for, a part of your "body" in the same sense that your foot and your hand and your gall bladder are all parts of you?

What parts of your physical body do you all not like? Does that mean they are any less parts of you or any less needed by your physical body?

What might "For he himself is our peace, who has made the two one, and has destroyed the barrier, the dividing wall of hostility.. His purpose was to create in himself one new human being out of the two" mean?

Safety from danger, harm and bad things as a natural, protective desire of God for all of us is very evident especially in the Psalms (see Ps. 4:8; 12:7; 16:1; 27:5; 31:20 and the verses surrounding these for examples).

God's power in providing safety is described in Proverbs 18:10 and 29:25 is described clearly. In John 17:12 as Jesus prays, he talks about "keeping them (those given Him by God) safe by that name you gave me."

Safety in childhood is absent for those who become multiples. The events causing us to multiply are foreign to God's concern for our care. One of the most interesting verses in Matthew is 18:10. Jesus says, "See that you do not look down on one of these little ones. For I tell you that their angels in heaven always see the face of my Father in heaven."

He has just finished his speech about children being the greatest in the kingdom of heaven. He has just finished lamenting that woe is what anyone who causes a child to sin is to be expected. In fact, such woe is to be expected that it "would be better for him to have a millstone hung around his neck and to be drowned in the depths of the sea" (Matt. 18:6).

While we think we'd **feel** better if have some of those who harmed us go through that experience, chances are they had no safety in childhood. Safety is the presence of healthy, functional love.

When we love God with all our heart and all our soul and have no other gods, and love each other as we love our selves, safety is a given. It increases as love for God increases--certainly if you haven't love for yourself, you'll be more likely to harm others. As you love God more, your ability to love your self more in a healthy way increases, unless your spirituality is dysfunctional, too.

Safety from the inability to love God and safety to be able to love neighbor (even persecutorial alters) as self, and to allow this love to increase is indeed a theme of God's. It relates to each and all of us in that as we allow this increase, leaving judgment and punishment to the Judge, our ability to increase love and the safety it brings in the spiritual and physical world increases.

Why do we believe God is responsible for our safety as children?

If people around us choose to live outside of God's expectations, and we experience trauma as a result, does God become responsible for their actions? If so, how? If not, why not?

What do each of you want to say to God about the safety you did not have when you were a child?

It's hard to believe in God all the time. If God is so good and great, how come God let all this stuff happen? How do I know God is real? Why should I believe God even cares? Where was God when I was growing up? Why didn't God stop that stuff from happening? These are all important questions.

Since each of us, and each one within us, faces these questions, they are asked over and over again as we mature into the wholeness to which God has called us. I know some people find our spiritual growth difficult. They want us--all of us-- to be in one place, and to move along a nice developmental path in a predictable way. Predictable. Non-disruptive to their process, non-threatening. No way!

Each self, as they wrestle with the inevitability of God's existence and love, will grapple with the questions in different ways and at different stages. Not everyone will have rock solid belief all the time. We will often find ourselves crying out "Lord, I believe, help my unbelief!" feeling as if we speak out of both sides of our mouth, wondering how we can be included in God's flock with this kind of two sided attitude.

I feel that insecurity about our belief in God is often healthy. Insecurity about belief is based on movement, on doubt and concern, on unhealed pain--just the stuff of which spiritual formation is made. It's like occasional wilderness moments that we can use to strengthen who we are becoming. It takes courage.

The courage to accept this natural, recurring insecurity and to allow selves their experience of it is healing. God desires interaction, conversation, questions, concerns, all the communication involved in resolving the crises of insecurity Belief brings. As each of us in us works that process, our wholeness in God increases.

Again, insecurity about how you believe about God is inevitable, just as God's existence and love is inevitable. The reconciliation of those is part of the growing and healing process.

What is the image of God that prevents us from being comfortable with feeling insecure about our belief?

What were Peter's experiences of insecurity about his belief?

Think about the people you know who are deeply spiritual and times when they might have had difficulty believing. Talk with them if you choose to. You may also use your selves for this. Write about how others describe their response to recurring insecurity about their belief.

Have you ever thought about what it must have been like for Paul to be Paul? Here he was, the Jew of Jews, raised to be a rabbi, devoted to the extermination of the Christians who threatened the security of his belief, and then he suddenly finds himself one of **them**. The very people he worked so hard to destroy.

Every day Paul faced the horror of his past actions. The many murders of many of the friends and relatives of the people to whom he preached. His own darkness, **his own private Jerusalem**: that towards which he marched resolutely in search of completion of his own salvation, likely in fear and trembling.

He could not undo what he had done. He obviously did not incur the expected penalty--in fact, he was forgiven for what he did. Though he undoubtedly faced those people, and though it is not written what it must have been like for him, he lived in the knowledge of the **fact** of his forgiveness by God.

How did Paul live through this? What might the process of his healing have been? The first was the experience of being struck blind. Not many people are ready or willing to undergo such a profound experience with Our Lord. I'm sure it got his attention. It created such a feeling state, such terror, that he could only be vulnerable to the supernatural process going on around him. He was confronted head on by his actions. He chose to believe what he was experiencing.

Then Paul made another choice, one that must surely have required daily action to maintain. He chose to follow Jesus, to accept the call issued. Don't you know he had to work on getting all of him to follow? What about all those years of rabbinical training, learning to be the Jew of Jews? Perhaps the effort required to take the actions is part of his reference to running the race to win the prize.

The reconciliation of Paul's horror came through his willingness to be healed, to accept his past as in the past, and to represent what he now believed with equal fervor, using the good he had learned from his past to help in the present.

How is horror redeemed by Our Lord? Think about the horror of the lives of the lepers and those possessed by demons (Matt. 4:24, 8:16, 8:28, 9:32; Mk. 1:23, 7:25; Luke 4:33, 8:27).

What do you do with horror in your own life? How is it healed?

When you think about yourself in terms of your life, how does what Paul experienced offer you hope?

Paul, again, is the champion of this concept. It may be because of his own life and struggles to reconcile who he was with who he became, or perhaps just God's own way of getting the needed message of reconciliation out. We, too, need people who have done it before us.

Reconciliation is making peace with someone. It restores trust and safety, allowing a refuge or harbor to which one can retreat. God's reconciliation with humanity came through the paradox of Christ's crucifixion and resurrection. Those who know Our Lord deep in their hearts become "ministers of reconciliation" by virtue of their living witness. They demonstrate God's reconciliation with God's creation.

We multiples are in need of reconciliation internally and externally. Much of the conflict that can render us unable to function comes from the prolonged amnesia and conflict internally. From selves separated from the comfort and reconciliation needed for healing. It is **not** necessary or good to learn all the trauma too quickly, or all at once. It **is** necessary to begin to pray for the healing of the trauma and to invite and move towards reconciliation with those selves who carry it.

People are healed slowly and constantly all their days, just as trauma continues all their days. The reconciling of God continues, too. We need that reconciling within and with God all our days, helping us become more and more in Christ's image.

What steps do you think reconciliation involves?

How can you let reconciliation be a process, one that may involve difficult feelings that do not just "go away" all at once?

What do you think reconciliation might feel like? How would it feel to feel those feelings?

A facet is a face or lens through which we view an aspect--it is a part that sometimes shows up by itself; in people, an "aspect of self" may be a separate self contained in the self that is very different from the rest or it could be characteristics of the whole self.

Talking about selves involves paradoxes, something that is and isn't at the same time. A paradox in Scripture is how Jesus Christ is human and divine at the same time. An aspect of the self of Jesus Christ would be His gentle side; another would be His fierce side.

When we think about aspects of self and Scripture, we can begin to look at God and all the aspects God has. Another way of thinking about this is the many separate characteristics God has, so separate that God is named by many names.

Each name represents some separate, strong, unique and valuable characteristic of God. We might not like all of them in terms of how we understand them (such as Exodus 34:14, Psalms 18:35), and they are still all God.

We may not like all the aspects of self the self we usually present has. I don't like an aspect of self in me, the host, that is impatient, sometimes abrupt. Each self is, however, unique and valuable even if as raw material for refining.

Each self within the self also has aspects. There may be the small child within the adult body who represents fear, or the strong adolescent self that wants to give up living. Each is a piece of the tapestry of your life, and each brings its own unique healing and power to your process.

When you read Old Testament literature, take the time to consider the aspects of God that may be named like aspects of your self. Think about how you as a whole self have aspects, and how each self within you is both an aspect of you and also has aspects of self within.

What does the phrase "aspect of self" mean to you?

How do you understand God as having different aspects of self? Think about God the preserver (Ps. 21:3-8), rock (I Cor. 10:4), defender (Ps. 18:35).

What aspects of your self as you know them do you like? Dislike?

How can your life benefit from understanding yourself as a group of aspects working together?

The ministry of reconciliation is another of Paul's themes. As a Jew called to preach to the Gentiles, Paul knew all too well the challenges of being the one to draw people together around a common cause.

He also knew the personal challenges of feeling and being divided internally: the warring between desires. Isn't that a lot of what you deal with? Don't you find that parts of you want to make choices in one direction while other parts want to go in the absolute opposite direction?

Multiples have internal "Jews" and "Gentiles" in many forms.

Selves experience differences in faith and beliefs, in values, food preferences, sleep patterns, recreational preferences. We qualify for being Greek, Roman, Jewish, Samaritan, free, slave, Gentile, male, female, doubting, believing, and even just wondering all in one!

Look up, read, and think about I Corinthians 12:13; Galatians 3:28; and Colossians 3:11.

Think about how everyone--whether a multiple or not--has to reconcile the different desires and interests in their lives.

How did Paul represent Jesus' attitude about diversity (Gal. 3:28)?

What was the force that reconciled Jews and Gentiles?

When Paul found himself struggling with reconciling his own internal drives and desires, what did he do? (Check out Romans).

Dissociation is when you are separate from what you are experiencing, whether it is not knowing it is happening, not feeling it emotionally or physically, or not being aware of the facts about it. It varies from just feeling sort of disconnected and "spacey" to total amnesia.

Association is being firmly grounded in the world right now, in behavior, emotions, physical senses, and the facts of an event. It is, in a sense, being in and of the world at the moment.

Spiritual gifts given through the Spirit (1 Cor. 7:7-11) include the message of wisdom, the message of knowledge, faith, gifts of healing, miraculous powers, prophecy, distinguishing between spirits, speaking in different kinds of tongues, and the interpretation of tongues. To experience these, a person is usually somewhat dissociated--lifted up, feeling the fullness of the Spirit. At the moment, you can't be too associated and be speaking in tongues or "praying in the Spirit"-- you are out of the way, standing aside from your self to let God do the work.

How exciting it is to realize that some types of spiritual growth make healthy use of an ability that is sometimes problematic! It is sometimes a good thing to do to back up and share the space in one's self with "someone" else: the Holy Spirit.

Whether the expression of a spiritual gift from the Spirit is calm and quiet and private or a little outrageous and public, the gifts themselves are dissociative. And if dissociation is something God uses to express God's power through people, then there **is** good in it. The trauma that caused ours was not good; the dissociation itself can be of benefit to God as a means to let the Holy Spirit work.

Describe positive worship experiences where you felt like you weren't quite there--maybe the music, or atmosphere just lifted you out of yourself to a different state.

What is the reason that God may need people to dissociate a little (or maybe a lot!) to experience spiritual gifts?

How does the knowledge that your experience of dissociation may benefit God's ability to work through you affect you?

It is written that God inherits the praise of people who have committed themselves to God. To have God inhabit one's praises is a awesome idea. God? Living in my thoughts? My words, my songs, my prayers? You've got to be kidding.

Many of us who are multiples find ourselves dealing with profoundly horrible events, with things done to us or that we have done or experienced that are repulsive, dark, and "bad." We might even label them evil. The opposite of praise is faultfinding. You can't do both at the same time. There is much to reconcile among many selves about who God is, how powerful God is, why God allows such horrible stuff to happen, and how we can ever face God given our lives.

I think God values the "wrestling" we do with these questions--it is certainly more attention than we often pay our Creator. It is far easier to write God off than to work though those questions and come up with answers that are perhaps fluid, uncertain. If I have been involved in such things that were so bad I couldn't even be present for them, how can I ever be close to God?

Praise. If you are willing to even consider that God inhabits the praise of His people (Psalms 22:3, King James Version), then praise God. Because if God inhabits praise, and you are praising God, God inhabits you--no matter what you have done, who you are, your past. Ask the parts of you that are committed to God to praise God, so that God inhabits those parts more and more fully.

Those places that God inhabits can not be inhabited by any other spiritual force, or ultimately by the darkness and horror of our lives. Not denial or repression, this praise, but how darkness is exposed to light and healed.

It's a guarantee given by God that when you spend more and more time with more and more of your selves in praise (I have teams that sign up on a rotating basis, figure out new types of praise, new things for which to give praise) you spend less and less time in faultfinding--of God, of your life, even of others. And this means you are more able to heal and increase your ability to function more as God intended you to.

When and how do you praise God?

What would it take for you to be willing to commit to a schedule of praise with a plan to evaluate what happens as a result of this activity?

Circle areas about which you can give praise:

Beauty	*Sunrises and sunsets*
Caring people	*Friends*
Determined clinicians	*Good sleep*
People who understand	*Food*
Medical care	*Sun, stars, moon*
Pretty flowers	*Air to breathe*
Toys to play with	*Pleasant voices*
Stuffed animals to hug	*Physical Safety*
Progress, even a little	*Times when you can laugh*
Creation	*Angels*

What are other things for which you can praise God?

There are many stories about abusive behavior in the Bible. In the Old Testament, you can read about incest, rape, sacrifice, murder, violence and abuse (physical, sexual, emotional and spiritual) over and over again.

Yet we also read of the loathing Jesus had for anyone who caused a little child to sin(Matt. 18:2-5, Luke 17:2-3), for not wanting anything except love. We read Old Testament laws that prohibit sexual contact between family members, confine sexual contact to those married to each other and as a consenting act between customers and prostitutes or concubines.

We read rules against much of the behavior we experienced as children, behavior that has indeed caused us to sin (many selves, in fact). To our horror, we realize we may have behaved the same way (after all, it is what we learned).

Injunctions about corporal punishment (which can be physically abusive) and the book of Proverbs seem contradictory. They seem to support an adult's right to traumatize children. Some adults may use these verses to justify the harm they do.

The question is: **What is God's position about abuse?** The first commandment, when followed, leaves no room for abuse. Our Lord said that the greatest commandment in the Law was "Love the Lord your God with all your heart and all your soul and with all your mind." He said "the second is like it: 'Love your neighbor as yourself.'"

When people live these two commandments, it is hard to see how abuse can occur. God does not seem to support or endorse abuse in the New Testament, and the Law itself does not seem to support abuse. Abuse opposes the mercy, compassion, and love of God. Its existence, a choice made by humans, invokes the justice, wrath, and anger of God.

As each of us continues to grow spiritually, increasing how much and how consistently we live out the two great commandments, we become less and less able to abuse one another.

How do you think God feels about abuse?

What do you believe Jesus feels about what you experienced?

If you believe that God does not support or want abuse, what are the reasons it happens?

Children have a hard time when abuse or trauma happens. They think, "If God really is a God of love and mercy, how come it happened?" And if it happens over and over again, they think God must be angry with them, or it wouldn't keep happening.

Sometimes people who hurt children make that easier to believe. They tell children that they deserve what is happening, or that God is punishing them. Those statements are not true. Children deserve protection from trauma and abuse; they deserve safety--the kind of safety that allows them to grow up without the scars that trauma leaves behind.

It is unlikely that God would send an adult to abuse a child as punishment.

God's anger, I believe, is more at the adults who lie to children, abuse children and make those children to do abusive things. We selves who have this in our lives wrestle with the horror of our own experience and what we have done as a result of it--become abusive ourselves--as we find ourselves seeking and trying to embrace the mercy God offers.

I believe God's anger is at the long chain of human behavior that gives people room to use each other in mental, emotional, physical, sexual and spiritual ways that do not line up with the two great commands Our Lord focused on.

How do we answer when we have become a person or when a self within is one of those with whom God can and perhaps is angry because we have been or are abusive towards children, internal or external, or towards others?

I answer guilty. And my heart breaks for those selves I know are and have been abusive, and my heart sings as I consciously choose to remember and require them to remember the mercy which God so liberally applies when each self owns its darkness and allows God to bring it to light and keep it there. Each time one of us is confronted with the opportunity to turn to the darkness again, we are stronger in the light of God's mercy.

What is the reason a child might believe God to be angry with them when they are abused or abuse others?

Where does Scripture address God's anger and its causes? (Use a concordance)

How can you help yourself learn to focus God's anger on those responsible for your trauma instead of believing God is angry with you?

Until a few years ago I would have laughed at what I am about to write. You might, too, and that's fine. It's at least worthy of consideration. I used--years ago--read about how "the sins of the father are visited on the children." I had no idea what it meant.

Then one day I was reading about the commandments handed down to Moses where God talks about blessing those who love Him (to the **thousandth** generation--Ex. 20:5-6) and cursing to the third and fourth generation those that hate him. It got my attention, and I checked out the cross references, reading the blessings and cursings list in Deuteronomy. I read, too, about the person in the New Testament where folks wanted to know what sin his family had committed to cause him such affliction, and Jesus said there wasn't one, that his affliction was there to glorify God.

Well. Suddenly I understood it all in a different way. Whatever sins my ancestors enjoyed and never relinquished or repented (turned away from to turn towards God) were like spiritual DNA. I inherited the vulnerability to the same class of sins as a result of their choices. It was up to me to choose: continue, passing the flaw on if I had children, or to clean it up.

I chose to clean it up. It only made sense: since the enemy prowls around like a hungry lion looking for easy prey, and since their stuff made me easier prey, I decided to intercede on their behalf and claim the rightful freedom Christ promises.

You wouldn't believe the changes in my life. By using binding up those areas, their aspects and attributes, and returning them to God the Father, Son and Holy Ghost for re-assignment as God so chose, and **then** asking Jesus Christ to loose in the cleaned out places whatever fruits and gifts of the Spirit as needed, my life began to make radical turns, with radical healing occurring in a short period of time.

I have had to **learn** how to maintain my hold on the good, since the bad tries to come back and take up residence. And I've made a commitment: no more inheritances from the enemy. I'll recognize them and root them out--as I am told I can, using the authority of the name and blood of Our Lord to gain my freedom. You can, too.

Circle sins you know about in your family over the generations:

Stealing	Lying	Deceiving others
Robbing neighbors	Taking another's life	Gossiping
Idolatry	Tripping the blind	Perverting justice
Favoritism, partiality	Incest	Harboring hate in the heart
Seeking revenge	Bearing a grudge	Holding back wages
Adultery	Endangering others	Sacrificing
Cursing the deaf	Divination or sorcery	Prostitution
Cheating another	Disrespect to elderly	Mediums / spiritists
Sex with animals	Hostility towards God	Alcohol/Drug addiction
Taking one's own life	Slandering others	Mistreating widows/orphans
Making false charges	Accepting bribes	Worshiping other gods

Circle the blessings you would like in your life:

Good weather	Peace	Freedom from Fear
Safety	Removal of enemies	Being fruitful
Plenty of food	Finding bargains	Experiencing God
Freedom from slavery	Work that satisfies	Happy children
Blessed work	Well thought of	Food lasts a long time
Enemies come, flee	Blessed travel	Blessed where you are
Abundant prosperity	Lend to many	Borrow from none
Made a leader	Blessed property	Respected by others

Circle the evidence of sin by others or by you that you'd like to avoid:

Confusion	Work destroyed	Wasting diseases
Inflammation, fever	Drought, heat	Blight, mildew
Defeat	Boils, tumors	Festering sores
Madness	Itch	Oppression
Being robbed	Broken relationships	Being unable to live in your home
Slavery		

What would it take for you to want to be rid of the consequences of the sins and to replace them with good things from God?

Psalms (Is. 54:4, 61:7: Zeph. 3:19) talks about how God will "turn our shame to praise." The first time someone pointed that out to me, I didn't even want to hear it. I've learned, though, to listen up when I respond to something that strongly.

So I looked up the references and began to ask internally what the reasons might be that the response was so strong. I found a couple of answers. If you have difficulty believing that God might turn your shame to praise, we might have some of these reasons in common.

The first answer I found came from looking up the word "shame" in what I call the "Exhausting Concordance" (about 8 pounds of it!). Strong's provides definitions of the words from their original Hebrew and Greek as well as connections to other words that have the same origins or roots or that are derived from the one you just read about. What I found was that the meaning of "shame" almost always relates to humiliation, and often to the humiliation of a woman and a man by exposure of their private parts.

Another reason my response was so strong was simple disbelief. As many times as I had been shamed and shamed myself, how could or by process would God ever turn that to praise? What a stupid idea! Simply, I doubted.

A third answer came from recognizing the strong judgements around shame both in the stories of shame in the Bible and in my own life. With as much judgement as was attached, how could the liberty of praise ever replace it? And what about God inhabiting the praise of His people? How did that reconcile with the issue of being filled with shame?

In the course of time, I recognized that God indeed transforms what was shameful and what each of us chooses to think and feel about them to events praise. Each moment of life we choose to keep on living in spite of our shame turns it to praise. Each time we allow the working of God in us in our healing to be an example of courage, strength, and vulnerability to God to others, we allow God to turn shame into praise. It's a conscious choice we make to risk letting God do what God does best.

If your shame were turned to praise, how would your life be different?

What role does modesty of different types play in reversing shame?

What are you doing to stop judging and start praising about your life?

Gentleness, patience, kindness. These spiritual fruits and the others (read Galatians to find them) require different thoughts, feelings and actions than do the spiritual gifts. To demonstrate them, you need to be connected to yourself.

Being connected to yourself means being in touch with what you're experiencing, or being associated. It means being aware of what you are feeling physically and emotionally, knowing how you are behaving, and being aware of the facts of what is happening.

It also means being connected to your will, or your ability to choose. In a situation where you feel impatient, it takes an act of will to think, feel, and act patiently instead of getting uptight and grouchy.

Being loving, joyful, peaceful, patient, kind, good, and faithful in more and more situations takes attention and intentional behavior. It takes more conscious effort than acting in ways opposite (hateful, sad, conflicted, impatient, cruel, bad, suspicious).

It is the choice to acknowledge these fruits in yourself (however green or ripe each may be!) and to begin to consciously live them out that calls on you to be in touch with what you are feeling, thinking, experiencing and sensing in situations.

Instead of getting out of the way of yourself like you do in dissociative states, here you are called on to **get in your way--to interfere with your reactions, those ways of being and doing that are the same things over and over again.**

That "getting in your own way" is one of the challenges of the selves that have responded "yes" to following Jesus Christ. It is part of becoming more and more like Him as you develop spiritually.

One of the exciting things about having different selves that are committed to Christ is that each will be in a different place of spiritual maturity, so that all can help each other grow--while learning to let the fruits of the Spirit mature and be evident in everyday life inside and out.

How is the process of having the fruits of the Holy Spirit develop like growing vegetables?

When a gardener refuses to tend to the plants and maturing fruits, what happens?

How do you tend your "spiritual garden"?

Spend time focusing on acting on the fruits God is maturing in you. It will take energy and effort. Then, describe how much more or less you switched or shifted and what that was like for you.

When something changes form, it is transformed. You might say that when we switch or change from self to self, we are transformed. When a person makes a commitment to follow Christ, they engage in a process of being transformed, of going from everything they knew that was familiar, comfortable and learned from living as we have to becoming people who live an unfamiliar, different, and initially uncomfortable lifestyle.

When you read the verses that talk about how we are to be transformed by our relationship with Our Lord, it becomes clear that this process re-shapes our lives. That doesn't mean it is always easy, just that the outcome is pretty incredible.

Romans 12:2 talks about being transformed through the renewal of the mind so that we can test and "approve" what God's good, pleasing and perfect will is. It takes a change in form, something which occurs over time and which has stumbles and even setbacks as part of the normal learning process, to begin to be able to recognize God's will.

Transformation is scary. It's a little dissociative in that you're letting go of and from who you were and a little associative in that your connecting yourself to someone you are becoming, an unknown. **It involves trust.**

As some point, each self and each person chooses to trust God as they grow spiritually. The transformation that has been occurring becomes complete enough to show the potential, and there is a glimpse of the "what might become."

Perhaps there is the overwhelming fatigue that says "I of my own self can do nothing (one of Paul's sayings)" and if you're really who you say you are and want for me what you say you want, you take over.

On the one hand, you can't make any progress with both feet on the ground. But you can't make any with both feet off the ground, either--so it means putting one foot in front of the other, participating in and allowing God to work away.

Being clay, and being transformed, is no easy task. The process is challenging, the result incredibly beautiful.

Romans 12:2   Do not conform any longer to the pattern of this world, but be transformed by the renewing of your mind. Then you will be able to test and approve what God's will is--his good, pleasing and perfect will.

2 Corinthians 3:18   And we, who with unveiled faces all reflect the Lord's glory, are being transformed into his likeness with ever-increasing glory, which comes from the Lord, who is the Spirit.

Philippians 3:21   who, by the power that enables him to bring everything under his control, will transform our lowly bodies so that they will be like his glorious body.

What do each of these verses tell you about being transformed?

How is your process of healing as a multiple transformational?

Someone asked me how I reconciled the passages about "singlemindedness" with being a multiple and healing. I said it was all up to God. God wants me singleminded with many more than one self, that's God's business. My job is conformity to Christ.

Many into one is important when you think of the many value systems your selves have. It's important when you think of the different and sometimes opposing spiritual choices, or when you think about opinions, what food to eat, which clothes to wear.

Is many into one important in healing? Yes. When all of you is rowing in the same direction, your life is easier. All parts of God--the Father, Son and Holy Spirit--row in the same direction. Jesus rowed in the same direction all the time: doing His Father's work. Peter, over time, got his "many" into "one" between his conflicts with himself. Did he believe or didn't he; would he stick with Jesus or not; he sure thought he'd be loyal, and he wasn't; he wanted to love and follow, yet he ran. The end of the story? He got his "many" sides all line up and working as "one" and ended up a powerful witness.

Again, my concern is conforming to Christ. What that looks like in terms of several selves or one is God's business. My job day to day is to live, serve, love, function and do well on God's behalf; to be healthfully diligent about the possibility of spiritual oppression and to fight against it, and to be vulnerable to what I believe I hear God saying.

As for many into one, may the Lord bless His intent for me and help me keep my eyes--all of them--on fulfilling God's will instead of trying to create it.

If all your focus is on integration, and afterwards you find yourself in a situation where forming an additional self is the healthiest choice, how might you feel about that outcome?

When you think about being "double-minded," what does that mean to you?

How is the concept of the Trinity--Father, Son, and Holy Ghost--both "triple-minded" and single minded?

How does that possibly apply to your healing process?

Go easy on it. That's the best advice I can give. Remember that the interior life is much more "see-through" than the exterior: often times very little is hidden from anyone inside, while we can go about outside and hide what's going on.

If you live what you know, and as each self gets better at living what they know about the love of Jesus, the evangelization occurs much more naturally. This isn't a situation where you can open the Word, preach at and to someone, act and sound holy, and walk away and go back to your old dark ways. That "someone" is internal and sees you fall back into those patterns that are far short of the commandments of Jesus.

Jesus said the two greatest commandments are "Love the Lord your God with all your heart, soul and mind; and love your neighbor as yourself." Evangelizing neighbors is best done by living a life that invites them to follow Jesus.

So it is internally. Be willing to ask forgiveness--more than an apology, it is hard to do and bears much fruit. Be willing to acknowledge God is still working on you, and practice doing what you can to live more and more of that learning out.

Be willing to praise God in spite of the challenges and problems; make praising God your foremost activity, stick with it, and watch what happens. It bears powerful testimony to alters who watch wondering why you would even bother to be a Christian.

Remember, too, many selves may have been abused by Christians and by the Church, and they may need to watch long and see if **you** are any different from the others. Love every part. Love some more. Give up self-abusive thoughts, feelings, actions; climb off the throne and put God there. Praise, and praise some more. Be like Jesus was: teaching, loving, praying, serving (here, serving alters first since they are always present), ignoring the put downs and jeers of people who didn't believe.

As you persist and grow, making this witness of life and deed to those inside, they become vulnerable to hearing about, considering and accepting Jesus for themselves. Over time, more and more of you is transformed, made new, and your wholeness reaches another dimension. Give it time. Go easy. Walk the talk.

What "turns you off" about people evangelizing?

How do you think selves inside will react if you do this to them?

How can you act differently towards everyone inside to show more of how Jesus loves and cares for you?

What will you do if they act like they don't care or believe you?

God has this habit of being merciful. Every day I start out with the best of intentions. Usually, before the day has ended, I've blown it--sometimes pretty badly.

Oh, my goal is good: love the Lord my God with all my heart, love my neighbor as myself. I can assure you, I'm embarrassed by some of the things I've called various "neighbors" and certainly wouldn't want to be loved like that (says how I love me at that moment, doesn't it?). Or maybe I've lost my temper and literally wanted to destroy something, or... Well, you know how it goes.

I keep a round rock on top of my computer monitor. It reminds me of what I deserve. Far as I can see it, "sin" only has three letters. It's one of the few places where I am pretty much an "either/or" person. Either is, or isn't.

Fact is, the sins committed against me during the times when I was becoming a multiple and the sins I've committed are no different. All are sins, all who committed them fell short of the glory of God, and all can be redeemed.

Ouch. Do I mean that the so and so who did such and such is just as important to God as I am? Do I mean that my Lord cares as much for them as me? How can He?!

His mercy is wide. Jesus Christ grieves as much for their sins as for mine, wants their redemption and restoration as much as mine, and doesn't wish justice for me any more than for them. Justice. That's what the rock is about. If I got justice, I'd get stoned. I get mercy instead--I do **not** get what I deserve under the law.

The wideness of God's mercy is in the challenge extended to us to want for our neighbors, even the ones who offended against us in abuse, what we want for ourselves. That mercy is so wide we can do it, trusting that in willing mercy towards them, we are less desirous of justice for ourselves.

After all, if it's all sin to God, why should they get justice when we get mercy? Mercy is freely obtainable through recognizing what we do that merits the justice we don't want, and asking for the forgiveness available to us through Christ.

Which would you prefer, justice or mercy?

Why do church leaders often want justice for some people and mercy for others?

What is it that makes it hard for you to want mercy for people who have hurt you?

How do you think Jesus would help you learn to have more mercy?

Why don't we like the judgements God makes sometimes?

I think forgiveness is God's specialty. Forgiveness is very different from an apology. It restores the situation, spirituality, to the condition prior to the offense. We have a harder time acting that out in the physical, making it "stick" as it were. It takes much effort to "erase" that time from our experience and let the healing occur.

An apology simply states there is regret about the event. It in no way restores the previous state. It leaves a barrier up, limiting the degree of healing that can occur. Read about forgiveness in Matthew 6:12, 6:14, 18:21-35. These span the Lord's prayer, how we are forgiven as we forgive, and the parable about how God deals with forgiveness.

Mark's gospel approaches it a little differently, talking in 11:25 about how if you hold anything against anyone, forgive him so you can be forgiven. That's hard to handle when others have committed atrocities, actions which would result in millstones around their neck in terms of Jesus' position. It's also contrary to human nature to ask for God to forgive someone who has nearly destroyed you, caused you to spend all this money and time trying to heal and who probably **looks** like they're getting off scot-free.

Sometimes doing the hardest thing is still the right thing to do. You do it for yourself instead of the other person, even though the cords of the event bind both of you. The reciprocity is in how both people remember, try to forget over and over the situation, and still carry the feelings and the resentment.

It is an act of will to ask for and offer forgiveness, one that you may need to repeat over and over, helping everyone release the event. It prevents carrying the burden of not having your sins forgiven as you have chosen not to forgive others, and begins to set right the relationships between people.

Try it with small, less overwhelming things first. Ask someone to forgive you for something you've done that you know wasn't right. Stand in front of the anger if it comes and ask again, "Will you forgive me?" Offer forgiveness as well--"I did not like how this happened, and I offer you forgiveness. Will you accept it?" See what happens.

Why might it be harder to say "Please forgive me" than "I'm sorry"?

How do you think it would feel if someone said "Please forgive me" instead of "I'm sorry"?

What might it take for you to begin to ask for forgiveness as well as apologize?

How might you resolve it if the person who was abusive is dead or doesn't want forgiveness?

No matter what book you read, you'll find some content you don't like or disagree with. Books open up whole worlds of ideas; they can give comfort and help you heal, too. However, I do believe in "GIGO." That means "garbage in, garbage out."

Box up or throw out secular books that contain stuff like what you lived through: inappropriate sexual contact, violence, horror, and graphic terror. The Bible has enough in it that is somehow redeemed for God's purposes to keep you interested and your adrenalin up for years (except when you read Numbers!). Get rid of the garbage and sooner or later you'll find less garbage coming out of your mind, mouth an heart.

To meet the reading needs of everyone, get books that cover a span of age level interest. There is a children's Bible story book that younger selves can enjoy, while older selves read adult Bibles. Teens may like a younger version of Scripture. Scholarly selves may enjoy a study Bible.

Read whatever version of the Bible you get like you would any other book. It has history, poetry, sociology, romance, war, adventure, and folk sayings.

Here are some authors who write interesting, easy to read books that will feed you as well as entertain you:
> Joseph Girzone (The "Joshua" series)
> Hannah Hurnard ("Hind's Feet on High Places")
> Madeline L'Engle ("A Stitch in Time")
> C.S. Lewis ("The Narnia Chronicles")

See if your local library has any of their books, and begin to enjoy them. If the don't local churches may have lending libraries. They may even have some videotapes you might enjoy.

What do you like to read?

How is it like or different from the trauma you experienced?

When you read for pleasure, what can you read that will help everyone have fun?

What do you all think you'd enjoy reading about?

How many books a month do you read?

Every part of you needs age appropriate prayers. It's interesting to listen to everyone as they pray, those who are young to older, those new in Christ to those more mature.

Many people set forth structures for prayer. All of them seem to contain several common themes:

> Giving thanks and praise for everything you can think of
> Confessing your sins or goof-ups
> Talking to or with God about them
> Asking for and accepting God's forgiveness for them
> Asking and telling God about the needs of other people
> Using the power God gives you through Jesus to fight spiritual oppression

Obviously, everyone will pray differently. Parts of me that grew up in a pretty formal Episcopal church pray one way; other parts more comfortable in less structured pray; and "Fanny Fundamental and the Fundamentalettes" do have what we laughingly call a "healing-and-squealing-get-down-good-time-with-Jesus!"

A good prayer for anyone is the Lord's prayer. Little ones can learn it from bigger ones, and bigger ones can explore the meaning and pray it different ways. Try praying about each line in it. Expand and tell Your Lord about what each segment means to you, and explain it to others in the system.

Children's books of prayers are fun, too, for ways to freshen up your prayer life. Writing your own with your own internal children helps them understand and value prayer. You can help everyone learn more about the nurturing and comfort prayer brings by making it more a part of your life.

It's a good activity to practice throughout the day, under your breath or to yourself. Sometimes you can even have internal groups praying around the clock. Pray about and for everything you see as you go about your day.

How often do you pray and for what reason?

Read some of the passages in the Bible about prayer (check out John 17 to see how Jesus prayed). What do they tell you about prayer?

Who in you likes to pray? Who would be willing to spend time praying?

What do you need from prayer? What are you willing to put into it?

There are times when I don't like God. I have, at those times, no interest in expressing joy in God. Sometimes I choose not to, and sometimes I choose to do it anyway.

I--and you--don't have to like God to express joy. We may be personally angry at what our lives have contained, blame God for it, forget God wasn't the only one involved. While joy may be just a goal for you, it can be achieved.

At the moments when joy is a far away goal, are the colors of a beautiful sunrise any less gorgeous? The smell of a flower in spring any less sweet? The miracle of an armadillo any less interesting? For those able to feel it, the hope offered by Jesus' death and resurrection any less majestic? In spite of how each of us may personally feel, the wonders are still there.

If we choose to let it, our joy can be there too. Taking joy in what God has put together (remember, the way it was intended and the way much of it still ends up) is healthy. It's a way to take a little more responsibility for your healing and for your life.

Joy is often a choice. Can you choose to love someone? To hate them? Yes. And just as you can choose those states, and which one you wish to engage, you can choose to engage "joying in God"---acknowledging anger at what has happened, wanting God to interrupt the way things **were**, change the way things **are** and guarantee the way things will be and still rejoicing in God and what God does in the world that is good.

In other words, quit blaming God for everything that happens. Remember the enemy of God has power too. People have choices. God set things in motion that way, and having given us the tools to live in love, doesn't violate the rules by which things run. We do.

Give credit where credit is due, and go on and laugh and joy in God and creation. You can feel joy--even if you have to learn how-- and still hurt over what has happened to you. You can enjoy God and still be angry at what you've experienced.

List ten things about which you can feel joyful no matter what--even if they're really ordinary, like "food to eat."

What do you let cause you to stop being joyful?

If you don't know what joy feels like, who can you ask for a description

What would it take for you to be willing to practice feeling what you think they are describing?

There is nothing--**absolutely nothing**--you may have done or experienced that God was not present, grieving with you about your involvement, and longing to pluck you away and comfort you. God longs to hide you under His wings and nurture you to health.

God does **not** want, enjoy, or appreciate your self-abuse in judging yourself for actions you took or in which you were involved that are horrible. This is even more true if you were acting under the orders of others with more power and authority than you had in the situation. Adults are responsible for what they make children do. It is **still** true if you chose it yourself or another part of you chose it.

Every minute that you hate yourself, another part of you, or God for what happened you are simply wasting your time and God's and increasing your pain. You can't go back and undo anything, and you're only recreating horror in the present over the past. Not a very efficient way to manage the pain and heal.

God would far prefer that people love God, love themselves in healthy ways, and extend the same amount of healthy love to each other they extend to themselves. Wretching your guts up (literally and figuratively) day and night over what you've done does not fit this description.

Asking God to forgive those who caused you to do these things, and to forgive you when you yourself (host or alter) chose to do them without pressure from others is much healthier. And then choosing to turn and praise God for bringing you out, committing yourself to a life of healing and love more than those acts represent, and beginning to spread that among selves and others is a much more constructive use of your time. It won't feel good at first. It will take ongoing conscious effort, just as if you were learning a new sport (you **are** learning a new skill). You will need to choose different thoughts, different feelings, and different actions, and make them a habit.

Healing the horror is not accomplished by giving in to it. It is accomplished by putting it in perspective, giving it over to God over and over again, and then behaving in ways that keep it behind you, compartmentalized when you're not working on it in therapy, and living in the present.

What is the reason you choose to hang on to the horror in your life?

What would it take for you to be willing to release it?

How do you think God handles horror? How did Jesus handle the horror of being tempted by Satan?

What are some ways you can combat the intrusion of horror in your life?

Many symbols given us as reminders of our faith have difficult associations. They have been used by abusive people--including Christians--to alienate us from what we want to believe wholeheartedly, that our God is a good God, merciful and longsuffering, patient, interested in our well-being, One who loves us deeply, and is the Creator and Maker of our universe, Ruler above all.

Digging around in the Bible produces a wealth of signs given by God as symbols for the people to use as reminders. The cross is foremost among these. The Church itself is also a sign.

Remember the Church is not Christ. In addition to a few letters difference, Christ was and is the perfect expression of God. The Church is a collection of people as wounded and damaged as we are, often exerting their woundedness against each other and those who are seen as vulnerable and weaker. Same stuff the world is made of--yet **not** Christ.

The cross as such is not the best sign of our salvation: it was Christ's triumph over death in the resurrection after the crucifixion. That is what everyone was waiting for. We just don't have a good, eye-catching symbol for the empty tomb.

Christ is as hurt by the abuse heaped on us by organized religion, churches, ministers, God-fearing Christians, and others as we are. He is just as grieved by the misuse of symbols given to remind us of God's commitment and caring.

Our Lord also expects us to reclaim the symbols, instead of letting our woundedness keep us separate from him. Reclaiming the church as God's is a large undertaking, yet as each of us refuses to allow the church to be abusive, or to marginalize us, requiring it to be accountable for its actions as the body of Christ, it will change. And as we refuse to allow spiritual oppression to keep denying us the comfort of the reminders of our faith, that oppression will also lose its power.

There are two simple tools that help accomplish these deeds: praise and prayer. Praise so that God may inhabit us more and more fully, and so that we will wallow less and less in our pain, and prayer so that we may more and more align God's will with our world.

List some of the symbols from the Christian faith that have been "stolen" from you.

Make a list of the reasons you have let someone or something else continue to have them.

What can you do to refuse to let that keep happening?

Healing from shame is the primary journey of the wounded heart. We end up shamed and shaming because of the issues we inherit, those imposed on us by those who have their own inheritance, and because of what we invite into our life.

Restoration is a process. There may be symbolic acts along the way signalling milestones; there is seldom only one result. It is the process of uncovering the areas and events of shame, wrestling with the emotions and events that result, figuring out how one is passing on the shame to others, and then beginning to figure out how to interrupt the process and begin to reverse it.

How does one get restored? If you're going to be restored, recognition you are separate or that you have separated someone else is first. It may be from a church, from someone you love, or from an idea you once held dear. After recognition of the separation comes, exploration of the feelings and the facts around the event causing the separation is required. Many people get stuck here, getting hung up in the feelings or accepting too little or too much responsibility.

Once a fairly accurate picture of the event, an exploration of feelings around it and its implications has occurred, it's possible to begin building bridges to restore people to connected relationships of caring. Accountability and forgiveness can be managed. Amends can be made. God's healing power can be planted in the middle of the situation to shade and protect as well as heal.

It requires a willingess to experience the feelings and the fact of the shaming. More important, it requires a willingness to be restored. Being restored is painful. It evokes feelings of vulnerability, of woundedness, and of pain. It is hard to face those who have hurt you or whom you have hurt. The benefit to restoration is the calm and peace that come with restoration. God wishes us to be made whole in the face of our shame, to be restored to our position of wholeness. God wishes it for each self in us, and for us as a whole self.

Dare we admit those places where we have shamed self, selves, others and God, ask forgiveness, face the possible sorrow, anger or pain? Dare we engage the process which God engages with us? As we do so internally, offering compassion to our selves, we become more able to do so externally.

Look up these passages: Psalms 23:3, 51:12, and 71:20; Lamentations 5:19-22; and Galatians 6:1-2. What do they tell you about restoration?

When you feel you have been shamed, what would it take for you to feel restored?

How come it is so hard to seek restoration of someone who has wronged you?

We are each learning to live by the truth--that is, by the light. It takes a fight, for the enemy of God would have us stay in darkness. We have our knowledge of what is, those situations where we can get photographs, news clippings, legally viable evidence. We have situations where we have no such evidence.

Much of life is based in doubt. We face the reality, the truth, that Satan comes to steal and to kill, to bear false witness. Whatever that enemy of God can do to cause havoc is his intent.

It takes a great deal of effort to learn to suspend what we once believed was truth (perhaps that our childhood was "great") which turn out to be lies or falsehoods. When the "truth" crashes in, it's painful.

Are we as willing to recognize the possibility of yet another truth? When we remember what we remember, creating the same physiological feeling as a trauma when it happened, are we willing to let it be rewritten over time? Maybe even to say "no, that's not what happened--I thought it was, and I'm not sure" or "It wasn't."

Most of us are too attached to being right, to holding fast to what we believe is so, to the point of heaping lies on top of new discoveries about former truths. I have injuries I thought others created. I'm not so sure any more. The way I remember things happening may not be exactly or even close.

Why do memories change? Cognitive errors--logical mistakes in thinking-- are like dominoes, for one. Think about that for a while. We get used to adrenalin rushes, for another, and do what is necessary to create them, even taking fragments of memory and expanding them to meet a real, physiological need. We get deceived, for a third.

All these are normal processes. Fight to keep learning the truth, and let it change, whether if it means the trauma was more **or** less.

How do you deal with the idea that some of your memories might change as you find new information from other parts of you?

What can you do to help reduce the shame that might come with finding out something wasn't the way tyou thought it was?

If you know someone who finds out new information that changes the way they told something, do you think that makes them a liar? Why or why not?

What do you think God thinks and feels about multiples accessing previously hidden information that may change the way we believe something happened?